Internet Marketing 101

A Beginner's Guide to

Internet Profits

By

Justin Southworth

Text Copyright © 2018

Justin Southworth

All rights reserved

Text may be reproduced in part with attribution to the author.

ISBN 978-1986015370

Legal Disclaimer

Before you scroll down and read anything in this eBook, you need to be fully aware of the following.

Income Disclaimer: This document contains business strategies, marketing methods and other business advice that, regardless of the results and experience of others, may not produce the same or even similar results for you. I make absolutely no guarantee, expressed or implied, that by following the advice contained herein you will make any money or improve your current profits, as there are an infinite number of factors and variables that come into play regarding any given business.

Primarily, results will depend on the nature of the product or business model, the conditions of the marketplace, and situations and elements that are beyond the control of the business operator. Then too, sadly, there is the operator of the business; ambition, intelligence, work ethic, experience of the individual, aversion to or propensity for risk—these factors and many more are part of the equation that results in failure or success or anything in between.

As with any business endeavor, you assume all risk related to operations, investment, and money based on your own discretion and at your own risk and expense.

Liability Disclaimer: By reading this document, you assume all risks associated with using the advice given below, with a full understanding that you, solely, are responsible for anything that may occur as a result of putting this information into action in any way, regardless of your interpretation of the advice.

You further agree that the author cannot be held responsible in any way for the success or failure of your business as a result of the information presented herein. It's your responsibility to conduct your own due diligence regarding the safe and successful operation of your business if you intend to apply any of the information contained in this book in any way to your business operations.

In summary, you understand that the author makes absolutely no guarantees regarding income as a result of applying this information, as well as the fact that you are solely responsible for the results of any action taken on your part as a result of this information. As with all books of advice, self-help, and information there is a basic, unstated agreement between author and reader: If you succeed wildly, I won't send you an additional bill to claim part of your profits; if you fail miserably, you won't send me a bill to cover your expenses. Fair deal? This book should be only one of a number of sources of education and training towards success in your business.

Now that we've got that out of the way, let's get on with the good stuff!

Contents

Legal Disclaimer .... - 3 -
Introduction .... - 2 -
The World Has Changed .... - 16 -
    Why You Must Choose YOU .... - 22 -
    Introducing the 3-Step Plan .... - 26 -
Step 1: Building an Audience .... - 28 -
    Five ways to effectively build your audience: ..... - 28 -
    Why You Need A BLOG .... - 38 -
Step 2: Building a Relationship .... - 41 -
    8 Proven Steps to Maximizing the Effectiveness of Your Freebies .... - 47 -
Step 3: Creating a Sales Machine .... - 53 -
    The Sales Funnel .... - 55 -
    The Hyper-Responsive List Group .... - 57 -
Are You Willing To Choose YOU? .... - 61 -
Getting Started .... - 64 -
Marketing Glossary .... - 68 -

Introduction

Every entrepreneur has the power to make an absolute killing on the Internet.

Yes, this includes you.

Whether you're an existing marketer in search of serious passive income, a part-time dabbler who just can't get consistent sales with your existing funnel or maybe a newbie with no experience and a lot of desire, you have the power to pull six-figure annual profit off the Internet as consistent and routine as clockwork.

In fact, there is only one thing that separates the wannabes from the wealthy, the tinkerers from the Trumps: successful Internet marketers have learned how to effectively and consistently **_DRIVE TRAFFIC_** in an ever-changing Internet world.

It sounds simple, right? It is. But don't confuse simple with easy. You will need to set yourself on a journey toward personal and professional education and development to which you must totally commit. But why should you believe me? What's makes me such an expert on the subject?

I've spent untold hours over many years studying not only business (yes, I even hold an advanced degree in business from a major university), but marketing in general and Internet marketing in specific. I've started business both on and off the Internet and have the failures to prove it. There is nothing about business, and especially an Internet business, that is a sure thing and the only sure-fire path to success is through failure. But through both failure and success I found certain principles that are immutable. I can tell you that everything you're about to read in this eBook WORKS. This is one of the most important skill sets you will ever learn.

This information can radically alter your personal finances for the better and, indirectly, your entire life. In life, as in most business endeavors you can generally have time or you can have money; having both is as rare as hen's teeth. Internet marketing is one of those rare business models that can give you a good income and the time to enjoy it. It will give you control, once and for all, over how to achieve your short and long term goals. As a tool for financial independence it will ultimately impact every area of your life.

As someone interested in Internet profits, you might very well have a goal in mind or some idea about what you want to do with this new-found knowledge. Maybe you just want to improve your marketing funnel. Perhaps you just want extra cash to put away for emergencies. Or maybe you want to earn enough to quit your current job and retire early.

Regardless of your intentions at this moment, I can tell you that as soon as you learn the skills I'm going to teach you, you are going to see immediate improvements in every area of your Internet marketing business.

Take a moment to consider why you do the things you do. What is the motivation that drives your actions? Why do you want to master Internet marketing?

Try this on for size. Is your thinking along the lines of, "Lots of people are making lots of money on the Internet. Why not me?"

But can't you also make a lot of money in a professional career? A career as a nurse anesthetist offers a mean salary of about

$140K on average throughout the United States (as of 2016). What about being a salesmen? There are door-to-door vacuum cleaner salesmen who make $100K per year. A good salesman with the right product can make a lot more than that.

So why isn't everyone knocking on doors and making a killing? Because not only is it difficult, there is no freedom in it. A salesman or nurse anesthetist, not matter how much they make, is still trading hours for dollars; it is IMPOSSIBLE TO LEVERAGE YOUR TIME AND EFFORT. As of the time of this writing you still can't clone yourself. In other words, even if you make $100 per hour, you still have a limited number of hours per day and hours per year you can work. Typically, careers that are the result of education and certification, where you're working for someone else, have a limit to their income potential. There's going to be a cap on your earning (profit) potential.

On top of that, even if you were a high-billing lawyer and could bill for your time sixteen hours a day, 365 days a year, would you want to? How long could you keep that up? Even with a high-paying job you're tied into a burdensome weekly schedule.

Of what use is having money if you can't enjoy it? Maybe you don't mind working 80 hours a week to earn the big bucks so your family can have a nice life. But there's more to providing for a family than money. You think maybe your children would like to have you around? As important as earning a good income is, freedom to enjoy it, freedom to do what you want on your own time, freedom to live and work wherever you want as much or as little as you want is equally important.

Don't get confused about why you are in college, or why you spent years in college or why you are working a salaried or hourly job (Notice I didn't say "career?" That would be redundant; a career is just a really l-o-n-g job.). Everything you do, you do for one of two reasons: to increase pleasure or decrease displeasure. Sure, some people say they like their jobs, but would they continue doing them if they did not need the money and if they were not paid for the work? Money is only a medium of exchange and we work so we can earn currency with which to trade for services and things we want. And really, consciously or unconsciously, isn't your goal to leave your job for good and have enough money to just DO WHAT YOU WANT?

Not having the skills you are about to learn—how to properly and effectively create lasting value for your customers and drive traffic to your business—means you won't know whether you're heading in the proper direction. Without this set of knowledge you really won't know whether you're making headway toward the ultimate goal: financial independence.

There are lots of people out there who just get "lucky," but we are not interested in that. Why would you want to be one of the lucky ones? Why would you want to be the person who just so happened to be in the right place at the right time in order for something good to happen to you?

I'm not going to teach you how to put yourself into routine strategies and systems that simply allow whatever happens to happen. I'm going to teach you how to CREATE the most profitable and effective marketing system. I'm going to give you a blueprint that will allow you to rapidly grow and scale your Internet business.

Everyone has heard "knowledge is power." It sounds good. It even sounds right.

But it is wrong.

Just having knowledge may be compared with having a chest full of cash. If you're on a dessert isle with no place to use the cash, it's useless. But if you are in a position to invest that cash, if you do something productive with it, then it can make a difference in your life.

You see,

Knowledge isn't power.

APPLIED knowledge is power.

You can know anything and everything, but if you don't apply the concepts, you will not be any more powerful.

Let's say, just for fun, that the information and methods in this eBook, if used properly to plan and build a rock-solid Internet business, could generate a million dollars per year. All you have to do is learn the concepts and follow the system and in a matter of time you will have a million dollars in the bank. (Whether the bank is the best place to put your million is a question for another book.)

When you receive this book, when you have this system available to you, are you rich? Of course not. Do you have a million dollars? No, you don't! (And for heaven's sake, don't count your chickens before they hatch!) Even after you read and study this eBook, all you have is the knowledge about HOW to get the million dollars. You have to motivate yourself, lay the groundwork, follow the plan, and then achieve the results. Knowledge is nothing more than a means to an end. You are learning this material for one reason—so you can apply it. If you don't put this knowledge to use you'll just waste valuable brain cells. You'd be far better off having a beer and watching another football game.

Are you still with me? Good. I want to mention a few more things about goals.

The human brain, among other things, is an intention-fulfilling mechanism. We have the innate ability to create an idea about something we want and then work toward achieving that end. Regardless of anything else, any external event, good or bad, we are always working toward the goals that we have created for ourselves.

As a result of this truth, it is extremely important to be aware of what your goals actually are. Your brain does not discern between what you might consider to be good or bad for you. If you imagine something, even better, if you speak something, your brain takes that as a command to somehow get that specific thing.

This aspect of the human psyche is hard-wired into our most basic, innate cognitive processes. Think about your goals as an Internet marketer right now. Take some time to figure out exactly what you want to gain by learning this material.

Go ahead. Take some time.

Here's what I'm listening to as I wait.
https://www.youtube.com/watch?v=dbfa86bTD34

Got it? I hope so. Be certain that it is something very specific. Speak out loud what you want to achieve, then write it down on a paper that you will put on your refrigerator door (so you can see it every time you reach for a beer). Then speak out loud and write down why you want that goal. You may want to keep the why to yourself, or you may want to post it together with your goal on your refrigerator. WHAT you want is not as important as WHY you want it. Why do you want to learn how to effectively market products and services on the Internet? Remember, all those people at Home Depot buying drills do not want a drill; they want a hole. Unless you're very unusual, you don't want to be an Internet marketing maven; you want the income and lifestyle of an Internet marketing maven. Why are you reading this eBook? You are much more likely to attain your goals if you can explain, and explain in detail to yourself and others WHY you want your goals.

Consider this very carefully. Tell yourself why you wish to learn this material. Let me be clear. Whatever you wish to gain from this, you WILL gain in some manner at some point. If you do not uncover your true intentions and set proper goals accordingly, you will probably not be happy with what you attain. Remember, the human brain is a coping mechanism that does not discern, but merely attempts to fulfill intentions.

KNOW and UNDERSTAND your intentions.

When I was learning the business, I thought I was very clear about what I wanted to get out of it. I wanted to be successful. The last thing I wanted was to be one of the seemingly massive statistics of people who fail at this business. But what I found out was that for me, just wanting success was not enough of a reason why and it was a rather poor excuse for a goal.

Therefore, I was not ready for some of the early financial success that I achieved. Financial success has a way of creating its own issues resulting in circumstances we least expect. As they say, be careful what you wish for.

So it goes with aspiring marketers more often than not. I've worked with many students who were not clear about their intentions from the beginning. They studied and applied knowledge and eventually found themselves at a point where they thought they wanted to be, only to realize that they weren't truly satisfied. Their goal had been to make money. But remember that chest full of cash on a desert isle?

If that is your intention, if all you want to do is make money, it will happen. But the problem is that the moment you achieve that goal, you won't have anywhere else to go. You'll have nothing else to strive for. Your success will be generic and hollow. You'll stall out and feel you've hit a ceiling.

There are lots of "experts" in this field—authors, consultants, marketers turned instructors, those who attempt to turn modest success into coaching businesses—who are not as successful at Internet marketing as they'd like you to think. They set out with the typical simple intention most marketers have: "I want to make some money". Now they have that ability, and they have some money, but nothing else.

Or worse, they hop from one trend to the next, never understanding how to create AUTHORITY, VALUE, PASSIVE INCOME and LIFESTYLE.

They can make a living but have no idea how to transform the knowledge of Internet marketing into a larger business or the wealth required to have true financial independence. Even if you're a full-time Internet marketer, if you don't do it right, if you don't do it smart, you simply trade one job for another.

Perhaps that doesn't sound like a bad idea—sitting around your house or condo near the beach pulling a living off the Internet. If that does it for you, then great! But you must be certain of your true intentions because whatever they are, I can assure you, they'll be fulfilled.

I know this from experience. I was one of those guys who just wanted to make money. Personally, when I hit that target, it was pretty hollow. I figured I needed to do more. More systems, more software, more everything. I thought I needed to spend even more TIME and MONEY to increase my bottom line. Had I realized that my true intentions were much larger—about the overall picture of personal freedom and financial independence—I could have saved a lot of time and avoided a lot of frustration.

I've worked with enough different types of personalities and preferences to begin to see patterns in behavior as well as business-specific patterns. These core tenets and strategies transcend time and "change." These are some of the concepts that I'm going to teach you.

The reality is that 90% of Internet startups FAIL in 120 days. And it gets worse. Statistical probabilities do not favor success for most because the entrepreneur is part of the PROBLEM.

Wildly successful entrepreneurs all exhibit the same characteristic: they are masters of time and resource management. I will show you how to do this. You will not achieve that end just by reading this eBook, however. You will need to combine the knowledge herein with sufficient personal growth and experience.

Maybe you're still not convinced. Are you still making the excuse that because you were not born with inherent talent or a ton of business acumen you won't ever be good at it?

Successful entrepreneurs are never born; they are always made. You see this everywhere. You may fall into some level of success, but without diligence and knowledge of how to make this thing work, you won't be able to sustain it. Remember,

Luck don't last.

It's so common as to be a cliché: one generation creates wealth, the next generation sustains it, and the third loses it. A talent for generating wealth is not in our DNA. It is learned. Some people grow up in an environment conducive to learning wealth principles, but that doesn't mean you can't learn whatever you need right now and apply it to achieve your own goals, no matter your background.

What I'm saying is that great marketers are not born with the ability to master the myriad necessary skills. All of these skills are learned. The skill set has to be acquired. And sadly, you won't be an expert by reading one eBook. You'll have to learn by doing. You'll fail and miss the mark time and again, but if you keep at it, with the correct knowledge, you'll eventually succeed.

There's a term in business called "barriers to entry." Simply stated, a barrier to entry is anything that makes it difficult to start a business. Maybe you'd like to build airplanes and compete with Boeing and Airbus, but there's a barrier to entry into that business, namely several billion dollars and years of design and manufacturing before you earn even one dollar in revenue. Not so with the Internet. Here, the barriers to entry barely exist. This is both positive and negative. It's phenomenal that average person can make above average incomes, but only if he or she understands key business structures and processes that consistently produce success among the millions of competitors who are also in the business partly due to the same negligible barriers to entry.

Many "natural" entrepreneurs acquire invaluable information by mimicking successful marketers. This may be the only thing that separates you from them. Just remember that these naturals may not know why they're doing this or that action. They're just blindly following a trail that someone else has blazed. When they get off the trail, as they inevitably will, they won't have to tools to get back on track.

In terms of evolution, being a natural is not an adaptive trait. It will not help them survive in the long run. High-flying Internet marketers hit the stratosphere and then crash all the time. Outcomes can be random. But long term success is grounded in the ability to create value and drive traffic consistently throughout your enterprise.

This is exactly how I have generated a seven-figure income in my career. And now you are going to learn how to have the same level of success by acting on a totally conscious level. You will be able to control your actions when it comes to the process or learning and implementation. You will therefore be able to control subsequent outcomes. That's exciting!

The concept of learning in this manner is so much more powerful than having a traditional "natural" ability or learning "naturally," assuming that's even possible. When things occasionally don't go as planned (and they will) or you hit a bump (and you will), you'll know how to fix the situation. Naturals in this case would be forced to give up and move on. There are lots of entrepreneurs and Internet marketers from the tech-boom in the early 2000s who are teaching elementary school today.

Me? I know I have the skills and the knowledge to adapt to ever-changing conditions.

Here is an example: most people drive a car without ever understanding how the car actually works. Only mechanics and engineers truly understand how a car functions. So, when your car breaks down, if you're not a mechanic, you must call someone who is a mechanic so they can fix it. But if you are the mechanic, you can simply assess the damage, make the repair, and quickly be back on the road.

Entrepreneurialism is a lot different from automobile mechanics, but learning how to effectively market is quite similar. If you understand the core Internet marketing "mechanics" you will be able to make repairs and continue on down the road, building your businesses more successfully than your competitors. (And you won't have grease under your fingernails at the end of the day.)

Use the concepts in this eBook to structure your business properly. Test out the systems on your own. I've tested these strategies hundreds of times over the years. Other entrepreneurs have learned these strategies and continue to test them. Up to this point I have worked out every possible kink that I could find. Over the years I've built dozens of business strategies based on the very principles you'll find here.

The best benefit this information can offer you is the ability to really make these strategies your own. Once you *own* them and discover not only their possibilities but their limitations, as you discover your possibilities and limitations, you'll become conscious of what is going on in your business and in your head. You'll be the quarterback who is able to read a change in the defense as the ball is snapped and adapts his actions to achieve success regardless of the opposition. That's a great place to be.

While you read, keep an open mind. The process and everything you are about to learn is going to change your life in ways you haven't even imagined yet. Herein you will find important tools for how to make a killing off the Internet.

The World Has Changed

And it will never be the same.

Ever!

Let's look at why you want to develop sources of income other than a job or single business.

Following World War II, Americans were flush with cash from the post-war boom. The *American Dream* was born, derived from a Fannie Mae government-backed mortgage program aimed at the well-employed middle class. It spawned the mortgage industry. Why live within your means when you could borrow for the dream house in the suburbs?

And then it happened. A concept that built the great American nation, "work and save," turned into "borrow and spend." Eventually the 15 trillion-dollar mortgage banking industry steam rolled the entire nation, promising a quick and easy solution to "keeping up with the Joneses."

This evolution was accompanied by the largest systematic banking intervention in history through the Federal Reserve. The more the Fed and Congress manipulated the money supply and interest rates, the more pronounced the inevitable boom-and-bust cycles became. Cheap money flooded the housing and financial markets, but the wildly-swinging boom and bust cycles created extreme riches for some and miserable failure for others, oftentimes based on nothing other than the "luck of the draw." Those who were at the right place at the right time when the Fed opened the money chutes and/or Congress decided to support one group of well-connected political friends would benefit. The less well-connected, of whom there are always many, many more, would bare the brunt of business failures.

Consumer spending continued to increase thanks again to the banking industry, now flush with mortgage interest profits and looking for new ways to get that money into circulation at interest. The introduction of extreme credit card marketing came next, and credit card debt went asymptotic. Virtually non-existent in 1970, credit card debt stands at over $1 trillion at the end of 2017.

It was a house of cards…

An unprecedented financial crisis rocked the world in 2008. (Interestingly, U.S. total credit card debt peaked in 2008, then dropped after the financial hardships of that period, but is now back to the same level as just before the Great Recession. We seem to have short memories.) The most notable component of this latest bust was has not changed; in the most recent as in every similar national financial debacle, the middle class was made to absorb the shock. Why? It collectively carries the largest tax burden and so is always the largest source of income for government to tax.

But this time the credit cards were maxed out and the unprecedented increase in home values was negated by second and third mortgages Americans were using at unprecedented rates to withdraw cash from their home "ATMs.". Post 2008, the job and housing markets did no better than to remain flat.

So what's left?

Increasing national debt.

The government-sponsored bail-out of the banks whereby newly created cash was used to pay interest on bank assets, keeping the entire industry afloat. Trillions of dollars were added to the national debt. The result?

The recession never ended for most Americans. Let's take a look at the numbers:

25% of American households say they are "just getting by" financially

13% are "finding it difficult" to get by

34% feel worse off than they did five years ago

Only 30% report they are better off financially than five years ago

And even a closer look...

The cost of higher education is making many Americans reconsider the traditional four-year education. The soaring cost of tuition is out-pacing inflation.

The American obsession with automobiles has raced to record levels. The average length of an auto loan is now 66 months, the highest level ever. More disconcerting is that 25% of all new vehicle loans originated now extend from 73 to 84 months. That's SEVEN years! The price of an average auto sale is now $33,560 with a record high payment of $479 even with interest rates lower than ever, due to an artificially low cost of borrowing as a result of Federal Reserve and government manipulation of the money supply and interest rates.

The borrowing continues on unprecedented scales. But meanwhile...

Home ownership rates are dropping. Only 64.7% of Americans own their own homes, the lowest level in over twenty years. As fewer Americans can afford to buy and are forced into the rental market, rents are on the rise, increasing 6.1% since 2008 on a year-over-year basis as of this writing.

The savings picture adds clarity. Twenty-six percent of Americans do not have a single cent set aside for emergency expenses. Sixty-seven percent have less than six months of expenses saved. Curiously, high wage-earning households with incomes in excess of $75K per year are no better off. Fewer than half (46%) have a six month savings cushion.

It gets worse. Thirty-six percent of Americans have nothing saved for retirement. Thirty-six percent have less than $1,000 in savings and in their checking accounts. Why? The cost of living of course. Government intervention favors inflation, targeting an official rate of 2%, although more reasonable calculation formulas put the rate at over 7% per year. Consider the long-term effects of an inflation rate of 7%: a person who retired in 1998 with a monthly income of $2,000 would today require a monthly income of $7,739 to match the purchasing power of twenty years earlier. Even at the government target of 2% per year, that person's $2,000 per month income would have to be almost $3,000 today. How many retirement incomes can keep up?

The bottom line is that the nation's wealth has been decimated thanks to the government's manipulation of the money supply and interest rates. And the big shocker: the only demographic that reported an increase in wealth since 2008 was the 90th percentile (the richest top 10% of Americans).

People are broke.

Rising income and wealth inequality has been on the increase for the past several decades; the trend is unlikely to reverse anytime soon.

The most likely scenario: the slow recovery from the 2008 Great Recession will continue to create inequality in the coming years as assets are drawn down to cover increased consumption costs.

And so you might be asking: "Is there a silver-lining ANYWHERE?

Yes. There is. Right here: despite all the statistics about what is happening to the masses, contradictions to the trend are EVERYWHERE! More people than ever have discovered personal freedom as well as financial success while real unemployment (or underemployment) probably exceeds 20% or more.

Contrary to what you might think, none of what you just read about the changing world is bad news. It's not good news either; it's simply the new reality. You can ignore the situation and hope it goes away or you can blaze your OWN path. It's time to build a rock-solid business that will generate passive income AND furnish personal freedom.

And your best bet for accomplishing this goal is to learn a system that has a proven track record of success. More on this in just a minute.

But first… you are going to have to make a choice.

Why You Must Choose YOU

The choice you must first make is YOU.

James Altucher said it best:

> *"Human beings are born pioneers. The rise of corporatism (as opposed to capitalism) forced people into cubicles instead of out into the world, exploring and inventing and manifesting. The ethic of the Choose Yourself era is to not depend on those stifling trends that are defeating you. Instead, build your own platform, have faith and confidence in yourself instead of a jerry-rigged system, and define success on your own terms."*

Define success on your own terms.

                    Think about it.

Not societal norms, conventional wisdom or whatever popular culture dictates.

Since the dawn of man's time on earth, the basic human drive has been to seek out frontiers. (Remember this? *"Space: the final frontier. These are the voyages of the starship Enterprise. Its five-year mission: to explore strange new worlds, to seek out new life and new civilizations, to boldly go where no man has gone before."*) Consider the great migrations, manifest destiny, crossing the Bering Strait, early European exploration, colonization, breaking the sound barrier, one-hundred story buildings, a walk on the moon, the Wright brothers and aviation, nanotechnology, splitting the atom, finite mathematics, the artificial heart. I could go on and on. It's everywhere in history. It's everywhere right now, right in front of us. There's an old story of a patent lawyer who declared in the late 19th century the U.S. Patent office should close, as there was nothing more to be invented. The truth seems to be attributable to an 1899 edition of Punch Magazine. In that edition, the comedy magazine offered a look at the "coming century." In colloquy, a genius asked "isn't there a clerk who can examine patents?" A boy replied "Quite unnecessary, Sir. Everything that can be invented has been invented." The humorous story clearly points to the foolishness of people who would believe that. It's no different today. No matter where we are on the evolutionary scale of inventiveness, the best is yet to come.

You can be part of it.

Even the Pilgrims chose themselves. The hallmark of the human evolutionary spirit has been to carve out our own path, our own method—our own truth.

Before it lost its marketing way with that creepy, big plastic-headed king thing, the Burger King Restaurant chain built a successful international brand around the slogan "have it your way."

It's time to return to that way of thinking.

Choosing yourself will give you the skill set required to go out into the world and dictate your place in it.

It isn't just about starting an Internet business because you want to make money. The choose yourself mindset must first be in place because it furnishes the self-mastery required to put yourself out there and build the rock-solid business of your dreams. You must consciously choose to do something, no matter how small or seemingly insignificant, each day to improve yourself and your situation.

Without a conscious decision to choose yourself, when setbacks occur, as they will, they may seem insurmountable and you'll be tempted to throw in the towel, thinking, "what's the use?" You will ultimately succumb to the eroding middle class mindset and settle for an ever-shrinking real (after inflation) income.

Choosing yourself isn't a selfish thing. It's not self-centeredness. What you learn is that grounding yourself first, deciding what you want and following your destiny derives from relative self-mastery. It's a foundation for attacking your goals and following your dreams from the perspective of a healthy, sane, complete sense of self. It's only after mastering yourself and creating the world you want to live in that you can help others.

This basis allows you to act in harmony with your environment and those most important to you. You won't burn out. You'll seldom be bored. Life won't get stale. In this respect, choosing yourself is the best possible precursor to not only creating a meaningful life, but also taking the best care of your family and others who are affected by the decisions you make.

It's the ultimate value creator. And value is the supreme metric. People will be drawn to you and what you offer. And they will gladly exchange money for it, enriching you AND them.

The divorce courts are full of people who thought they were choosing themselves. They thought they were following their own path and walking their truth. But they weren't. All they did was buy into some canned conventional "dream" without ever knowing who they are. These are the people who wake up one day, look at the husband or the wife, the kids, the house, the pressure, relentless financial obligations, college tuition, debt, the $800 Lexus payment and think, "I'm DONE."

If you develop the mindset that you and you alone are responsible for carving out your place in the world, you can then focus on the idea that creating value will open up all the doors you need.

And that's when the money starts rolling in. Trust me. It will.

After I learned this, at every turn in my career and business evolution I chose myself. I wasn't even aware of it at the beginning. The reality is that the choices I made for myself were ultimately choices made for my family, my future, my way of life. The foundation of my entire life rests on that very first choice: I can tell you first hand, it WORKS. One of its greatest benefits has been the ability to guide other entrepreneurs in the proper direction.

      Think you are ready to choose?

           Then let's get down to business.

Introducing the 3-Step Plan

Let's simplify the process by beginning with the bottom line.

If you want to make six figures annually on the Internet, you are only going to require two things:

A Desirable Offer

and

Someone to Buy It

It really is that *simple*. But as I said earlier, it's not *easy*. With that said, most people make the process much more difficult than it has to be.

If all you do is focus on this simple structure of ***offer + buyer*** everything else will fall in line.

Remember that the only difference between Internet millionaires and those who never make a dime is that the millionaire was able to get lots of people to purchase a product or service.

Let's look at how we are going to work with this structure using a **3-step plan**:

1. **Build an Audience.** All successful businesses are built on the foundation of establishing, engaging and expanding a community with similar interests. Think of this audience as your 'tribe.'
2. **Build a Relationship** with that audience. People will know, like, and trust you enough to do business with you.

This is the foundation for creating AUTHORITY. The result is social proof.
3. **Create a Sales Machine** to offer high-quality, valuable products and services to your audience.

Now let's examine each step of this process in more detail.

Step 1: Building an Audience

Always remember this fundament truth:

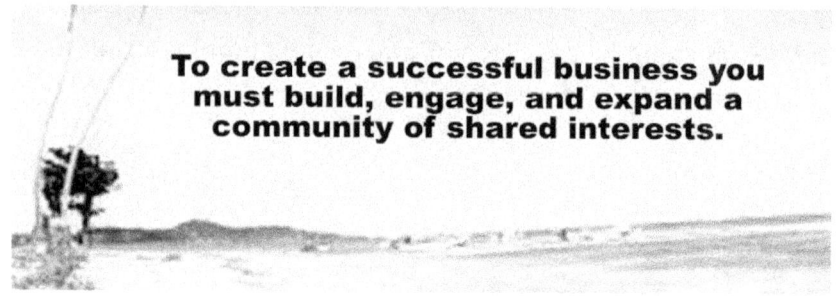

Five ways to effectively build your audience:

The first thing you need is access to the email address of everyone in the world. (That's an example of Internet Marketing humor—pretty lame, no?) But Rome wasn't built in a day, and you can start with a much smaller quantity. Your list is a tiny database that contains at first only subscribers' email addresses. As you develop your marketing savvy you can build this information into a relational database to rival FaceBook. But before that happens, you really can achieve a lot with just several hundred email addresses of willing subscribers. These individuals have "opted in" to your newsletter or other email offers. They willingly and (hopefully) enthusiastically agreed to receive communications from you on a regular basis. Typically, you will create a free offer to entice people to join your list. You will have to provide something of sufficient value in order to do this. Then you can begin to send follow-up emails to your subscriber base. Of course, you must get your initial offer in front of a potential subscriber. That's done through one, some, or all of the methods below.

1. Blog. This is your journal, a site on the Internet where you post content on a continual basis relevant to the interests of your target market. A blog is superior to a static website because, for one thing, frequent updating and 'backlinks' facilitate improved rankings in search engines. More importantly, *Content is King*; without up-to-date <u>interesting content</u> your readers will have no reason to return to your site. You only have to keep in mind that there are about a billion web sites floating around the ether. A user has to find yours, then he or she has to want to return. Remember, your blog is your main portal for establishing your personal VALUE and AUTHORITY.

2. Video: Using popular sites such as YouTube, you can create and post videos on a "channel" that people can subscribe to. Again, your videos have to be relevant to the interests of your target market. Your videos can demonstrate new products, you can give reviews of products and in your humorous and personal style, and you can give updates of new or upcoming products that will be available through your web site. It should go without saying that if you're going to produce videos they should present a professional view into your business. The video itself doesn't have to be made with professional equipment, but your presentation needs to be rehearsed and well presented. Rambling talk, poor sound quality, grammar and word choice that indicates you may have had better things to do than attend school,

all are killers to your video marketing efforts. It's outside of the scope of this eBook, but before you begin producing videos, so some study of at least the basics of producing video should be on your to-do list.

3. Podcasts. This technique involves offering a regularly-posted, downloadable audio files. Generally, podcasts are scheduled weekly and, again, cover topics of interest to your target market. Distinct from videos, podcasts are better suited to content that does not include any visual information. (Makes sense, right?) Interviews, updates of what's new in your industry, opinions, and series of educational content are all popular podcast formats. As with videos, a series of podcasts establishes you as an authority in your field.

4. Social Media. Here your goal is to create a "following" on platforms such as FaceBook, Twitter, Instagram, and every other social media site frequently used by your target market. Don't overlook FaceBook fan pages. You can establish a fan page for your business specifically to attract "friends" who want to keep abreast of the content you provide. Your fan page will stick to specific business topics and not veer into pictures of kittens of what you did on vacation, unless kittens and vacation stories are germane to your business.

5. Paid advertising. Methods 1-4 are basically free marketing venues. You may be able to build a large client base with those alone, but at some point you're probably going to want to take advantage of better targeting to a much wider audience that paid advertising provides. You can send emails with links to your product pages through sites such as Udimi.com, or you can pay

for advertising through social sites such as FaceBook, Twitter, Pinterest, and others. Again, an in-depth discussion of using paid advertising is out of the scope of this eBook, but there are more books and web sites available to provide information and instruction than you can ever use.

Using all five methods is not required for some level of success, but before you reach the top of the Internet marketing mountain you'll probably develop some not-too-shabby expertise in each one.

But as we've said, the money is in the list, so I'm going to spend a little more time and bits on list building through email and your blog site. Your list is the foundation of your Internet empire. Using the tools I'm about to provide, you can be up and running and collecting email addresses today!

List Building

The cornerstone of effective Internet marketing is the development of the email list. This is how you will be able to achieve high customer retention and high lifetime value.

What most marketers overlook is timing. Email address acquisition AFTER the sale is too late, because it requires the customer to pass through the current sales funnel and pay wall first. Therefore, your list will only be composed of paying customers.

But what about the "tire-kickers?" What about potential customers who are either curious or simply shopping?

You don't to miss out on ANYONE who expresses an interest in your niche. Think of it as an opportunity to introduce yourself, provide VALUE and demonstrate your AUTHORITY. And just because they didn't buy the first time, or buy that particular product doesn't mean they won't buy the next. Many people shop and think incessantly before making the decision to buy. The last thing you want is for them to forget you exist.

From this perspective, you must always build your list first. If you learn one thing from this entire blueprint, it should be this: *the money is in the list*. (I know. I said that. But education experts tell us that until you've heard or read something three times you don't remember it. I think that was the third, so we'll leave it at that.) You shouldn't consider your list as part of your business; you should consider that the list *is* your business. This same phenomenon can be seen in all sales and marketing, not just Internet marketing,.

If you're a plumber you'll notice the same people at the supply store. If you're a carpenter, you'll see the same people over and over at the lumber yard. If you're a regular at Starbucks, or any coffee shop, as I am, you'll eventually notice that you see the same people there time and time again. Like me, they also make it a daily habit to stop for their favorite drink. (Tall dark roast with a little room for cream.) This group is part of the millions of people on the Starbucks list. It's that sector of current and potential customers that are most likely to purchase from Starbucks in the very near future. If they don't buy a new French press today, they may buy one tomorrow or next month or get one for a Christmas present. On the Internet, where you don't have a physical store, your email list is basically the same thing as that group of Starbucks enthusiasts or the plumbers and carpenters who frequent the plumbing supply or lumber yard.

With this in mind, let's examine my primary list building strategy:

- Build an email list PRIOR to sending traffic to a sales page.
- Provide VALUE in exchange for the email address (This is generally an information product such as an eBook or video course). We will discuss this "freebie" next.
- Create a SQUEEZE PAGE to give away the product and capture emails. (Alternately, you may simply provide an Opt-In box on your website or a blog.)
- Run traffic to the squeeze page or blog, both of which have an email sign-up form.
- Locate affiliate products to promote according to your pre-determined FUNNEL.

I will be discussing the funnel later in this blueprint. But first, we need to cover sequences and an overview of the tools just mentioned so you know exactly what to do.

The Follow-up Sequence

Sequences are the series of emails with which you will correspond with your new potential customer once they have joined your list. Email auto-responders provide the tools to automate the process.

Keep in mind that from the very beginning, you want to provide VALUE and demonstrate AUTHORITY. To do that, concentrate on two areas:

- Content
- Frequency

Content is your message, what you want to introduce to or discuss with your prospects. You want to communicate valuable, reliable information with a frequency that does not allow the members of your list the opportunity of forgetting who you are and why you are writing to them. Your newsletter, your blog, and your videos should be packed with useful information. On top of that, an occasional free gift, also appropriate to your product offerings, should be part of your strategy.

Tools

To facilitate your list building initiative you'll need an autoresponder service to first collect email addresses and then email your follow-up sequences.

Remember that this is all automated. Time-based email scheduling will enable you to engage each new list member with your follow-up sequence beginning on the very first day they join the list.

You can find several email autoresponder services with a quick Internet search. My favorite is AWeber (https://www.aweber.com/), but there's also Mail Chimp, GetResponse, and Constant Contact to name just a few. Check them out. To help decide which one to use, get reviews from newsgroups or social media. It's difficult to know which one you'll prefer until you take them for a test drive, but by then, if you've built a good list and used their tools, it's difficult to change. Prices vary, but don't go with one or the other simply based on price. Remember, the *money* is in the list. Don't be a tight-wad; it's a small investment.

Once your email autoresponder is in place, you'll require either squeeze pages (also known as landing pages) or an opt-in applet to collect the email addresses.

Here's an example of a very basic squeeze page with an opt-in applet attached.

> **FREE VIDEO: Discover How You Can Test Drive The System That Took Me From ZERO To $9,000+ A Day!**
>
> Enter Your Email Address For FREE Instant Access...
>
> [Enter your best email address]
>
> [**Click Here To Watch The Video Now**]
>
> 🔒 Your Information is 100% secure.

Most autoresponder services have tools for building and customizing squeeze pages and opt-in boxes. (There are also squeeze page plugins for WordPress, if you have a website and use that software. I use Instabuilder (Instabuilder.com), which interfaces easily with AWeber.)

I'll cover some more detail about list building when I discuss blogging later in the eBook. This has been a brief introduction to the concepts of list building and follow-up sequences as well as the tools required to facilitate these strategies.

Let's review the benefits of this strategy:

- You build strong, LIFETIME VALUE across your enterprise. Now you have the possibility of repeat customers because you have earned the trust of your subscribers.
- You create exceptional VALUE by delivering timely, pertinent information to your audience, information your list subscribers cannot find elsewhere. (Well, hold on a

minute. That's actually a bit of hyperbole. It would be very difficult if not impossible to provide anything—information, product, or service—that your subscribers cannot find elsewhere. What you want to do is develop AUTHORITY so your subscribers trust the information that comes from you and a competitive advantage so that your subscribers don't actively seek the information elsewhere. There's nothing new under the sun; your challenge is delivering something old in a new package in a way that makes it seem new, or showing your subscribers how they can "scratch an itch" in a new and more effective way.)

- You achieve solid CUSTOMER RETENTION rates.
- You build a rock-solid, long term business…by first building the LIST

I've made as much as $75,000 in just a few days with targeted email marketing. The secret is found in the promotion of higher priced products further down the sales funnel. You'll be learning the best way accomplish this objective later in this blueprint.

Why You Need A BLOG

In this chapter, I'll discuss one of the most important tools available to successfully create the powerful long-term Internet business you've been learning about in this blueprint.

That tool is the Blog.

Think of a blog as your home-base on the Internet. It is a powerful communication portal connecting you to the world, a place where you can connect with customers and potential customers, a destination that gives you the power to introduce your business to the world, educate potential clients about the benefits of what you provide, and establish your authority.

The blog enables you integrate social networking and traffic generating tools and, most importantly, it allows you to build your list.

Through your blog you employ the proper mix of content, marketing, and monetization to create authority. When you build an authority blog and combine this with a large email list, you have a viable business entity that can be further monetized and even sold later.

Your blog must have a professional layout and constant theme that makes it a viable commercial entity. Therefore, how the blog is initially setup and structured is very important to your success.

As if there weren't enough pitfalls for most aspiring Internet marketers, the learning curve for successful blogging is sufficiently steep that many newbies and professionals alike are deterred from blogging and miss out on a huge opportunity to create a high-traffic business.

An authority-style blog layout will enable you to effectively build a list with an email opt-in applet to collect email address and further introduce customers and potential customers (leads) to your business and provide the entry to your sales funnel.

A properly-established blog only requires the following:

- Web hosting
- Domain name

For hosting, I recommend **GoDaddy** (https://www.godaddy.com/) because it is affordable, reliable, and includes every service you could possibly need to build an Internet business of any size. Plus, and most importantly for the beginner, their customer service is second to none. GoDaddy also includes a 1-Click WordPress install, so you can easily install your blogging platform in only a few minutes.

Here's a great video on how to start a profitable blog on GoDaddy using WordPress:

https://www.youtube.com/watch?v=_ci8AClHBog

If you're new to Internet hosting and WordPress, I suggest watching the entire video and completing each step on your own blog as you follow along. That way you can have your blog set up correctly within a couple of hours so you can start posting content and take the first step toward your goals. Remember:

- The journey of a thousand miles begins with the first step, and

- Beginning is half done.

Now that you are familiar with the tools of list building and the blog, let's examine how you can effectively build a rock-solid relationship with the new members recently acquired on your list.

Step 2: Building a Relationship

Let's take a look at another fundamental business truth:

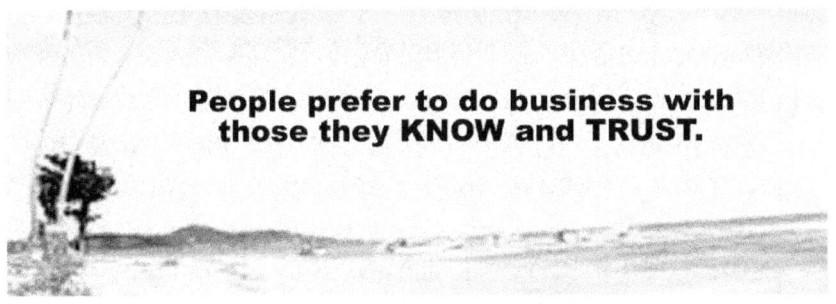

It's proven that you'll get higher conversion rates (sales) on offers to your existing audience (subscriber list). Put another way, conversion rates through advertisements to cold prospects will always underperform compared with marketing to a list of people who have willingly opted in to your emails.

This is why it is imperative that you establish a quality relationship with your audience. Please keep one very important thing in mind: in sales, you are NOT trying to get someone to accept your product in exchange for their money. Read that sentence again. (Just in case you didn't, I'll repeat it; you are NOT trying to get someone to accept your product in exchange for their money.) That raises the question, then what are you doing in the sales process?

I'm glad you asked.

> A salesman does one thing: He or she provides the information conduit between a product or

service and a person who needs or wants that product or service. Think of it like this—a person needs or wants something but he doesn't know where or how to get it. A salesman helps that person satisfy that want/need and for his services earns a commission. Or sometimes, the prospective buyer doesn't know he has a need, so another objective of the salesman is education. For example, we've all heard the expression, "He could sell ice to an Eskimo." On the surface that seems silly. Why would an Eskimo want to buy ice? Maybe the Eskimo doesn't know that rather than chop ice out of a glacier and carve it into cubes of the right size for his Tequila Sunrise, he could get them premade, which would allow him more time to spend with his pet seal. Along comes a salesman and offers the Eskimo a bag of pre-made cubes of just the right size and purity for his favorite breakfast drink. The Eskimo now realizes he has a desire—pre-made ice cubes. He didn't realize he wanted those because he had no idea they were available. Now that he has the information and can relate it to a desire to spend more time with his pet seal, he suddenly can't live without premade, crystal-clear ice cubes. Did the salesman manipulate the Eskimo into buying something he didn't want? Nothing could be further from the truth. The salesman was simply a conduit for new information that gave

> the Eskimo information he previously lacked. Given the new information, the Eskimo decided the ice cubes were worth more to him than the sale price and an exchange was made. Suddenly, both the salesman and Eskimo are better off. The free market is a wonderful thing!

Back to our method.

The easiest solution is to provide a high-demand freebie first as a lead magnet to attract new prospects to your list. Once there, you will continue to offer freebies inter-mixed with offers and promotions as a way to create value and build the relationship.

A freebie will enable you to:

- Introduce your expertise to your audience.
- Promote offers to your audience.

A great tactic for the second bullet above is to use a "blending" technique to position promotional offers inside free value-driven content. You will be able to engage your audience with ways to address their pain-points while offering solutions with products and services that generate revenue.

Some of the freebies I have used over the years with solid success are:

- Articles and blog posts. Combine like subject matter articles and posts into an eBook Articles and offer it as a bonus with a sale or just a freebie for goodwill. This can be of just about any style or about any subject. Some ideas are how-to, overviews, tips, tactics, strategies, or anything else you can imagine, as long as it fits into your business. Know your audience; once you produce a few articles or blog posts you'll begin to develop a style. If your audience enjoys your style they'll want it to continue. To change from being an information-based, "just the facts ma'am" kind of a writer to a snarky man-about-town may lose you some readers. On the other hand, if you are not gaining readers and subscribers, maybe you should consider changing your style.

Reports or white papers. These are similar to articles but are normally more structured and can be much longer. A report or white paper of twenty to twenty-five pages is not at all unusual. These typically deal with a new technology and offer the very interested reader an in-depth analysis of the technology, pros and cons, and future potential. If you're thinking of writing your own white paper or report, it's not something you'll dash off in a day or two. Plan on spending time in research and writing a high-quality document. Prospects who absorb the content and find it useful are very likely to become or remain long term clients or customers.

- Toolkits. This freebie makes it easy for your prospects to take action on the information they've been learning about. For example, a business start-up toolkit might include templates for fliers, mailings, sales forms, and invoices.
- Webinars. Your audience will place a high value on live events. This makes webinars an attractive freebie. The

added benefit is that recordings of webinars can be used over and over as marketing and education tools. If you cannot manage a webinar on your own or lack sufficient content, you may explore partnering with an affiliate and promoting the webinar. Promoting a webinar, done right, can result in equal benefits for your business as well as the producer of the webinar.

- Case studies. This is a presentation of a situation, a presentation and analysis of various tactics to correct the problem, what was actually done, and an analysis or "postmortem" of the change. Of course, the main idea here is to present a real-world example of a problem and how your product or service improved the situation, with the idea that your potential customer should purchase your solution. Case studies are used all the time in Internet marketing. You see them in splash pages for practically every product you look at. These are fine, and they're necessary. But you can also use a more refined, subtle, professional approach with members of your email list. Sometimes you want to hit 'em over the head to get their attention; other times you want to use a little more *savoir faire*.
- Email courses. I know several marketers who specialize in autoresponder email courses. The benefits of multi-part training segments as a freebie is that you do not have to create all the content before you can deliver value to your audience. Furthermore, over time you will be training your list subscribers to anticipate your value. For example, you could produce a ten-part e-course called "The 10 Secrets for Quickly Tripling Your Internet Traffic," sent via autoresponder on a schedule of one to

two segments per week. Another idea would be to include a link to the next segment the use can click on when he's finished the current one. Free training is always appreciated and links to products that help the user achieve objectives of the training that you also profit from is not a bad way to generate a little business.

- Cheat sheets. I use cheat sheets all the time to condense a more complex task down to a manageable procedure. Usually just one page, cheat sheets are downloadable, printable PDFs that provide exceptional value. They are also evergreen—usable for the long term—and may be included with other offers or as additional content in your autoresponder. Any document created with MS Office, Google Docs, or other major "office-type" software can be saved as a PDF and distributed to your readers. By so doing, no matter what type of computer or software they use they'll be able to receive your content.
- Newsletters. Probably one of the best tools for interacting with your audience, newsletters are normally sent on a weekly basis, but that's entirely up to you—twice a week, every two weeks, whatever is best for your target market. The important thing is consistency. Content can vary; one issue might involve training, the next could be an entertaining human interest story. Industry news, product reviews—any subject that allows you to intersect with the interests of your target audience and promote your business interests is a valid topic. Autoresponders provide newsletter templates so each issue has a uniform appearance. Set up the template once, then add content for each newsletter. Autoresponders also allow you to schedule publication dates

so you can create a series of newsletters once a month, for example, and have them sent weekly.

There you have it, a complete list. Really? Not on your life. Your imagination and creativity is the limit to the type of product you can offer to generate interest among your subscribers or potential subscribers.

In order to make the most of the freebie, you will need to know a few things first before you decide which strategies to use and how to structure your campaigns.

8 Proven Steps to Maximizing the Effectiveness of Your Freebies

- High-Quality Content: Don't imagine that just because you're giving something without charge that it doesn't have to be a high-quality product. This may be the first product your potential customer receives from you and you only get one chance to make a good impression. The freebie doesn't have to be gold-plated, but it has to something that indicates a respect for your audience. Plastic whistles were fine for Cracker Jack prizes, but those were for children. Put some time and thought into what you're giving away. Make sure it's useful and has some value for your potential customers.
- Make It Useful: Your freebie must be something that your audience is would actually want. How do you know what your potential customers want? Research. You must know who you are dealing with so you can properly engage them and offer something of value, something that will improve their circumstances.

How to conduct market research is a topic for an entire book, and I recommend you read a few if you're serious about your Internet marketing business. There is also enough information available online to keep you busy all day every day just doing research. Check out sites such as SimilarWeb.com, Compete.com, MonitorBacklinks.com, RankSignals.com, SEO Spyglass.com, and Ahrefs.com just to get started. Your auto-responder will probably allow you to include surveys in your mailings. You'll want to use this from time to time; people love to give their opinion.

- Make It Personal: Start seriously studying promotional emails you receive and internet ads. You'll probably notice that many include a face with the content. People prefer to do business with people they know—let your audience get to know you by first including a picture so they can attach your name to your face. If the tone of your newsletter is friendly and personal, your picture should reflect that attitude. On the other hand, if your newsletter is serious and pure business, think of an economic analysis or other serious subject, your picture should be formal, as if taken by a professional portrait photographer.

  You may also want to add a few tidbits about your everyday life, likes and dislikes, where you just went for vacation, or other personal details that will allow your clients to know you just a little. A little information can go a long way to building a bond and give your clients the feeling that they know you.

- Empathize: No one likes to be *sold* anything. High pressure sales gimmicks and over-the-top offers will not build the bond you are seeking for long-term success. Your audience needs to know that you understand their pain points and have a genuine solution.

  Let your audience know that you are aware of how they are feeling or where they are on a specific journey. Perhaps you have been there yourself. Empathy is the ultimate connector. When your clients see you as "one of us," you'll increase your credibility.

- Social Proof: This may be the most important tool in your arsenal. A testimonial from a client or from others who have utilized the product you're promoting is one of the best ways to build your brand and expand your influence. The Internet is filled with bogus offers, extreme promotions and unbelievable stories. Your clients know this. Honest reviews and testimonials will set you apart and give you much needed credibility. They should be specific and include details about the products features and benefits and how someone was able to achieve a certain, specific goal with the product.

  The case studies can be considered a type of social proof. Like a testimonial or review, it should include product features and benefits, but the emphasis is on an actual situation where someone had a need and was able to fill it with the product you're promoting. If you're not familiar with case studies and if you're serious about your business, pick up any copy of *The Harvard Business Review* and read one of their case studies to get an idea of how they're written. You can find plenty of case studies elsewhere, but the HBR includes one in each issue and they are well written. You won't go wrong modeling your case studies after theirs.

As an example, I recently conducted a case study for traffic-generating software using a small group of clients who had recently purchased the product. This focus group provided specific details about their traffic generation needs and problems and how the software improved their businesses during the two-week testing phase. The case study was then published in a newsletter specifically aimed at promoting that product.

If you cannot conduct your own case studies, you can find existing case studies in your industry or niche available on the Internet. Just make sure the case study is available for republication. To find these and other articles and eBooks you can redistribute, search on PLR or Private Label Rights. There are tens of thousands of documents available for free or a very small charge that you can use in your business.

- Engagement: The importance of proper engagement with your audience is crucial to your success as an Internet marketer. Always answer questions and respond to comments promptly, and make sure you add information with your response, not simply restate something already in the article being responded to. Empathize with your readers; they don't have the specific knowledge you do. Teach, direct, and encourage your audience.

If one of your list members is the catalyst for an interview, training segment, or newsletter topic, be certain to include their name in the process. This builds loyalty and makes you accessible. I work with one marketer who uses this tactic all the time. He does a weekly question and answer segment in a newsletter where he personally responds to a subscriber's question.

Schedule time each week to respond to questions and comments so this activity doesn't become something you do if you "get around to it." One of the most demoralizing things you can do to a member of your audience is ignore him or her. You would be surprised at how often this happens with Internet businesses. Marketers are so busy marketing that they forget the most important thing of all: the needs of their audience. Some of the most successful marketers and content providers I know have a policy that no question goes unanswered.

- Maintain a 3:1 ratio of freebie to product promotion as a general rule and don't overdo the number of emails. Carefully consider the amount of your total interaction as well as a ratio of free content to paid promotions. It has been proven that high *un*subscribe rates comes from two things: over-promotion and excessive email frequency. I have personally unsubscribed from lists because my email inbox was consumed with their emails. Regardless of whether there was good information in those emails, I just didn't want fifty percent of the first page of email to be from one sender each day.

If the only time your audience hears from you is when you have a new promotion or some other product for them to purchase, they will tire quickly and begin to suspect your business. In truth, everyone knows that your intent is to sell products, but marketers and customers have an unspoken but sacred contract: They agree to pretend that we are not just trying to make a buck if we fulfill our part of the contract by providing valuable information and treat them with the respect they deserve.

As a general rule, for every one product promotion that you send to your list, offer two freebies or just send a correspondence (email) with only valuable information. This doesn't mean that your signature shouldn't include a link to your site or to a specific page with a product offer. At any time some of your readers may be in the mood to buy something that you've advertised before. Maybe they deleted that email and so lost the link to it. You do not want to pass the opportunity to allow a client to purchase something. However, there's a difference between a link in your signature and an email actually promoting a product.

Now that we have studied how to maximize the relationship with our list, let's move on the most exciting part: building a sales machine that benefits from all the work we have done to this point.

Step 3: Creating a Sales Machine

Now we come to the part you have been anticipating: monetizing your business. We want to take the shortest path to turning the list and a good relationship with our audience into six-figure annual revenue.

The best way to do this is by creating your own products or partnering with content creators whose products fill a key desire of your clients. What you will be doing is building an electronic *funnel* that includes a variety of products at various price points to engage your audience at wherever they are most likely to commit financially.

The process begins with the freebie and graduates successively through a series of higher and higher-priced products. As your audience continues to get to know and trust you, they will commit greater amounts to purchasing these products.

At any one time, you will have a group of devoted followers who truly respond to your content. This group is worth gold. In a coming chapter I will show you exactly how this funnel works.

For now, check out some examples of how you can achieve your financial goal of a six-figure income.

1. Create a $27 a month membership site. You'll need 310 active members to earn $100,440 per year.
2. Sell a $77 video training info product. You need four sales per day to make $112,420 per year.
3. Provide a $197 "done for you" (DFY) service. You need ten sales per week to make $102,440 per year.
4. Create a $997 webinar. You need 17 sales per webinar and six webinars a year to make $101,694 per year
5. Set up a $4,997 private 12-week coaching program. You need 21 sales to make $104,937 per year

Not that any of this is *easy*. Creating quality content never is and some of these ideas, numbers four and five especially, will require experience and the ability to teach and motivate. But as you will see in the next chapter, the process can be *simple*. And there are plenty of ways to earn a good Internet living without having to personally interact, meaning face to face, with your customers. I'll show you exactly how to take consistent, month-by-month steps to improve conversions, get more and more traffic, and add products to your funnel. In fact, some of my students have used the exact same funnel you are about to learn to build million-dollar Internet businesses.

They didn't have any special skills or expertise. Neither did I when I began. Virtually anyone can do this.

So, I hope you're excited and ready to take action!

Let's learn all everything we need to know about a funnel.

The Sales Funnel

In this chapter we'll expand on the concept of the funnel I mentioned earlier in the eBook.

Examine the following image:

The sales funnel model works in any niche market. The products in the funnel address the needs and concerns of your prospective customers. They are interrelated and each addresses a similar problem, providing a solution or educational material to resolve the needs of the buyer. The products in the funnel normally begin with the most basic, creating interest or in some way educating the buyer to the possibilities lying ahead, or in our case, further down the funnel.

Key point: Your initial marketing copy should only address the features and benefits of the initial product in the funnel. Whatever claims or promises are made in your initial customer contact, the sales page your email will lead to, have to be kept in the initial product. There can be no *bait-and-switch* here. That's the most efficient way to lose all credibility. Not just some, *all*. Not just sometime in the future, but *immediately*. If you promise a turn-key method to increase sales, then the initial product must deliver a turn-key method to increase sales. The customer should not receive a part of the product, only to find he has to purchase the next product in the funnel to have a complete system.

This funnel of products and services in the proper sequence has several benefits:

- It introduces your concept or idea in a way that requires a minimum of financial commitment on the part of the potential customer. It may even begin with an offer of something at no charge; this is the freebie you give away in the initial contact with the potential customer, normally through an email.
- With the first product, free or low cost, your customer is introduced to your business and your brand. He or she sees the quality of your offering. After this, you can introduce him or her to a follow-on product from a position of reliability and authority. Now the customer has justification for believing in your brand—the initial

barrier to spending his hard-earned money is a little lower and he's willing to take the next step toward a more feature-filled or convenient product.
- Each step builds confidence in your product offering on the part of the customer and gives you another chance to establish a closer relationship with him or her as you send helpful newsletters and product reviews and offers.
- As customers move through multiple funnels, each containing related products and services addressing a similar business challenge, they benefit from the more advanced solutions provided, and you build a reliable, profitable brand.

The Hyper-Responsive List Group

As your business expands, whether you are promoting your own products or affiliate products and services, there will be a select group of customers who will become your raving fans and love what you have to offer. They'll readily purchase virtually everything you promote because you have earned their trust by providing sincere value. (Naturally, this assumes you only produce or promote high-quality products with real value.) This same group will proceed through each funnel, seriously considering your more profitable products and will buy based on their trust in your business.

These people are your *hyper-responsive* list group. These customers create high lifetime value because they will purchase products and services at the bottom of the funnel.

This is where most marketers make the mistake of only promoting cheaper, niche-introductory products. Selling a thousand $17.95 products is nice, but selling a hundred $1,795.00 products goes a lot further in making your business a going concern for the long term.

Remember:

> Use the free products and less expensive products at the top of the funnel ONLY to INTRODUCE your expertise and create value in the mind of your customer and (*have we mentioned this before?*) to **BUILD YOUR LIST!**

Also remember that the funnel is a model that virtually any business can and does use. It's not unique to Internet marketing, but it is the most powerful concept you can employ in building and sustaining your business.

Before we close, I want to present three ways to increase your business. I wish I could say these were original ideas, but they're so basic no one can really claim credit. However, basic as they are, they are worth keeping in mind. Vince Lombardi used to hold a football in his hands and say to his team at the first meeting at the first day of each year's training camp: "Gentlemen, this is a football." No matter where you are in your business, keeping the basics in mind is goal number one.

Your business grows by:

1. Getting **more** customers. Continually build your list and get more targeted traffic by tracking and testing all your campaigns and landing pages. Find the words and phrases that pique the interest of your audience so that you're converting more of your browsers to buyers.
2. Getting **more** customers to spend **more** per sale. Increase revenue and increase profit per transaction. You can do this by offering upsells, cross-sells, and one-time offers on your order form. This is the purpose of the funnel.
3. Getting **more** customers to spend **more** per sale **more** often. The key to large profits in your business is incentivizing your existing customers to buy from you repeatedly. That's why it's so important to building product funnels. You always want to be presenting fresh

ideas and new products and services to your hyper-responsive list group.

Now let's condense everything into one easy, actionable plan you can start implementing TODAY!

Are You Willing To Choose YOU?

Believe it or not, you now have the foundation to build a wildly successful Internet business. It's not easy, but it is simple. Perhaps some of the details are fuzzy, but that's okay. The point is that from the perspective of structure, you know exactly what to do:

- Build an audience…
- Create a rock-solid relationship with that audience…
- Build and expand a round-the-clock sales machine with sales funnels...
- Take the process step by step, day after day, building your business like a brick layer builds a massive wall.

You can imagine your six-figure business at its completion, but do not be overwhelmed by the process it will take to get there.

I am going to give you a specific starting point – right now. You can start today to build the business of your dreams by doing this…

Build one list with

one source of traffic by offering

one freebie or targeted offer.

Pretty simple, no?

Use the tools mentioned earlier in this eBook. If you take this first step you will have a list provider so you can begin to collect email addresses for your future funnel.

Each day, every month, take one step closer to completing your funnel. This could be a new product, finding a new source of traffic to add to your list, or even adding a new freebie to your autoresponder to create more value and build your relationship and brand.

The choice to begin TODAY is a choice for you. Will you do it? Or will you make an excuse to put off your Internet business for another time?

If you begin today you will be amazed at the progress you have made in a year, six months, or even three months.

Your focus on list building will drive your business as you find out how to fill the needs of your audience. You will learn their pain points and what products and services will improve their lives.

You really can "sell ice to Eskimos." Find a need or problem and find a way to fulfill it or fix it. Let the world know you have their solution. Become a problem solver to the masses.

It remains the most powerful strategy I have ever seen. I can tell you it works. I have done it. I'm doing it right now and I'm teaching others how to live their dreams.

If you apply everything you've learned in this eBook and use the information I've provided, you will achieve great success on the Internet. You now have a proven SYSTEM.

There is no need to struggle any more with trial-and-error or hit-and-miss Internet marketing opportunities.

It is time to choose *you* for all the reasons I've suggested in this eBook. It's about defining success on your own terms, carving your own path and creating a lifestyle for you and those you care about.

Getting Started

If you're like I was when starting out, even after reading everything I could get my hands on concerning the topic of Internet marketing, I still wanted someone to take me by the hand and lead me through the process of getting my business off the ground. There are people who will do that—for a price. Nobody works for free. (And if you find that for free, consider that you get what you pay for.)

However, I can present you with the startup steps so you can create your plan. Just as a brick and mortar business needs to put together their infrastructure and processes before they can open their doors to the public, an Internet business needs to put a lot of things in place before broadcasting its presence to the world. Here are the steps you'll need:

Even though a lot of products you'll see advertised say you don't need a web site to make money on the Internet, in my experience, I've found that not to be true. Eventually you'll want your own branded web site so you might as well get one now. It's pretty inexpensive to register a domain name with **GoDaddy.com**. Buy their most inexpensive hosting package and build a basic site with **WordPress**. The video referenced above will show you how to do that.

So, step one is get yourself a web site. Think carefully about your domain name because you're going to eventually broadcast it to the world and once you've started your business you won't want to change your name unless ABSOLUTELY necessary. You'll find that many of the names you think of are already registered, but with some creativity you'll find a suitable name.

Consider using your own name, as in JohnSmith.com. (That one's probably taken, but it's just an example.) You can then put your marketing pages and blog in a directory under that, as in JohnSmith.com/FreeThing.

Get an account with an auto-responder. As I've mentioned, I prefer **AWeber** but you have more options than you can shake a stick at. If you want to just keep it simple and you don't mind taking some free advice, get an account at AWeber and move on. They'll give you everything you'll need to build any size business. I began using their services because they were highly recommended by an Internet marketer I respect. I haven't been disappointed.

Find a product or two or three you can give away. Search the Internet for PLR to find eBooks and reports, or write your own. If you already have a product you can give as a freebie, so much the better.

Eventually you'll want (maybe need) to use paid advertising, but you're also going to want a presence on every social media outlet that might possibly link you to a customer. Again, there is more free information on the Internet than you can read in a lifetime on how to build networks on Facebook, Twitter, Pinterest, LinkedIn, and every other social networking site in existence. Make a habit each day of developing as many friends or contacts on each site as humanly possible, but don't start out with advertising. As I said before, there's a game we play, a little dance in Internet marketing. We pretend we're not interested in selling a million dollars' worth of products a year and the audience pretends that they don't know we just want to sell a million dollars' worth of products a year. Yes, I'm being just a little tongue-in-cheek, but making a business of using social networking sites to promote products is a whole different animal from hanging out on Facebook and watching funny puppy videos. Your intent will be to let the world know what you have for sale, but you can't make it *obvious* that this is your goal. And even if you don't really enjoy hanging out on Facebook and Pinterest, you'll have to do it anyway. Post intelligent responses to other people's posts. Ask questions. Engage others. Make yourself useful. Collect friends and contacts. This will take some time, but it's free exposure that will pay benefits in the future. Over time you'll be able to slip in some ads, and if you've built up a loyal following, those ads will be seen and acted upon.

Now you've got your web site, you have something to offer for free so you can start building your list, and you're a known quantity on several social networking sites. If you're planning on building a business with affiliate marketing, you're going to need a product to sell. **JVZoo.com** is a great place to start to find products to begin with. They have tutorials on how to set up an account and become an affiliate so I won't bother repeating that information here. If you already have a product to sell or an Amazon store you can skip that and go right to the process. Upload your free report or eBook to your web site, set up a squeeze page either on your web site or through your auto-responder (both work, but I use a plugin on my WordPress site called **InstaBuilder** that interfaces very easily with AWeber), test and test and test again to make sure everything is working as expected, then start letting people on your social network sites know that they can receive something of value absolutely free and without obligation at, for example, YourDomain.com/Free Gift.

As I've said, you'll want to keep in contact with the people who have signed up on your list. Your blog can serve dual duty here. (You're posting relevant and useful information at least weekly on your blog, right?) You can set up your auto-responder to broadcast your blog page as an RSS feed, or you can copy the blog post into an email to be sent by your autoresponder at a time of your choosing. Remember the 2/3 rule: two out of three correspondences with the people on your list should include useful and timely information. In general, only offer something for sale in one out of three. Links to products (if you have an Amazon store, for example) don't necessarily count as promotions. As you write your newsletters and promotions, think like a consumer. Remember, you're a problem solver, not a salesman or saleswoman.

There you have it, a step-by-step start to your Internet marketing business. They say the devil's in the details, but in this case, I think it's better said "the angel's in the detail." The constant learning about new and more effective techniques and products should be enjoyable. If it's not, you're probably not going to be very successful. It's true, this business can make equal money with others with much less time, but it's not as if you can set things in motion and then forget it. It's not plate spinning either, but something in between. I sincerely hope you enjoy your journey!

Here's to YOUR success!

Internet Marketing Glossary

Note to readers: Many of these definitions borrow heavily from Direct Online Marketing, (https://www.directom.com/) but a definition, by definition, is simply a definition, not subject to creative license, at least in my humble opinion. I have limited the verbiage to the minimum required to define the term and have made additions and corrections where necessary. You can find out more about any of these terms by searching on Direct Online Marketing, Wikipedia, Google, Bing, and other Internet locations.

Above the Fold - The part of the page you can see without scrolling down or over. The exact amount of space will vary by viewer because of screen settings. You often pay a premium for advertisement placements above the fold, which will add to the costs of internet marketing services, but may also add to results.

adCenter - Bing Ads powers paid search results on Microsoft's Bing, Yahoo! (as of November 2010), and other sites within its network. Bing Ads was formally known as Microsoft adCenter.

Ad Extensions - Added information that is included in your text ad. These can include extra features about your business, such as your location, phone number, links to certain product or services pages, and call-outs.

Advertising Network - A group of websites where one advertiser controls all or a portion of the ads for all sites. A common example is the Google Search Network, which includes AOL, Amazon, Ask.com (formerly Ask Jeeves), and thousands of other sites. In Google AdWords, they offer two types of ad networks on the internet: search and display (which used to be called their content network).

AdWords - AdWords is Google's paid search marketing program, the largest such program in the world and in most countries with notable exceptions such as China (Baidu) and Russia (Yandex). Introduced in 2001, AdWords was the first pay per click provider offering the concept of Quality Score, factoring search relevancy (via click-through rate) along with bid to determine ad position.

Affiliate Marketing - A type of internet marketing in which you partner with other websites, individuals, or companies to send traffic to your site.

Aggregate Data - Data that details how a group of consumers interacts with your marketing efforts or websites. This can be how an audience views videos, ads, pictures, etc. and what actions are taken after viewing. This can give a comprehensive view of how your target market is engaged, as a whole, through marketing efforts, as opposed to individualized consumer data.

ALT Tags - HTML tags used to describe website graphics by displaying a block of text when moused-over. Search engines are generally unable to view graphics or distinguish text that might be contained within them, and the implementation of an ALT tag enables search engines to categorize that graphic. There is also talk that business websites will all be required to utilize ALT tags for all pictures to comply with certain American Disability Act requirements.

AMP - An acronym for the Google-backed Accelerated Mobile Pages Project was announced by Google in October 2015. It was designed as an open-source initiative for publishers to create content that loads quickly on mobile devices. AMP consists of three parts: AMP HTML, AMP JS & Google AMP Cache. For more information see the AMP Project website (https://www.ampproject.org/).

Analytics - Also known as Web Metrics. Analytics refers to the collection of data about a website and its users. Analytics programs typically give performance data on clicks, time, pages viewed, website paths, and a variety of other information. The proper use of Web analytics allows website owners to improve their visitor experience, which often leads to higher ROI for profit-based sites.

Anchor Text - The clickable words of a hypertext link; they will appear as the underlined (usually) blue part in standard Web design. In the preceding sentence, "hypertext link" is the anchor text. As with anything in SEO, it can be overdone, but generally speaking, using your important keywords in the anchor text is highly desirable.

Astroturfing - The process of creating fake grassroots campaigns. Astroturfing is often used specifically regarding review sites like Google Places, Yelp, Judy's Book, and more. These fake reviews can be positive reviews for your own company or slander against your competitors. Generally frowned upon, to put it mildly, by ethical Internet marketers.

Automated Rules - A feature in Google AdWords that automatically adjusts your ad statuses, budgets, and bids based on the specific parameters that you set.

Average Position - This statistic describes what position in which your ad typically appears on the search results page.

B

Backlinks - Links from other websites pointing to any particular page on your site. Also called Inbound Links. Search engines use backlinks to judge a site's credibility; if a site links to you, the reasoning goes, it is in effect vouching for your authority on a particular subject. Therefore, Link Building is an incredibly important part of Search Engine Optimization. How many links, the quality of the sites linking to you, and how they link to you all are important factors in ranking your web site on search engines.

Baidu - Serving primarily China, Baidu is the largest non-US based search engine in the world (although it was started in the United States). Sites can be optimized for Baidu and they offer their own paid search service.

Banners - Picture advertisements placed on websites. Such advertising is often a staple of internet marketing branding campaigns. Depending upon their size and shape, banner ads may also be referred to as buttons, inlines, leaderboards, skyscrapers, and other terms. When using specifics, banner ads refer to a 468×60 pixel size. Banner ads can be static pictures, animated, or interactive. Banner ads appear anywhere on a site. Banner costs vary by website and advertiser; two of the most popular pay structures are Cost per 1,000 Impressions (CPM) and flat costs for a specified period of time.

Beacon Technology - is a form of technology that allows companies, primarily retailers and marketers, to connect and engage wirelessly with consumers via their mobile devices. The appeal is that companies can use the Bluetooth signal to deliver geo-targeted, personalized messages, and push notifications when the customer is in range of the beacon, and can even act as an analytics tool to decipher steps taken to reach a purchasing decision.

Behavioral Targeting (BT) - Behavioral targeting tries to put ads in front of people who should be more receptive to the particular message given past Web behavior, including purchases and websites visited. The use of cookies enables online behavioral targeting.

Bing - Bing is Microsoft's search engine, which replaced live.com in June 2009. Bing results now power Yahoo!'s search for paid (except display; through Microsoft adCenter) and organic (except local listings) through an alliance between the two companies.

Bing Ads Editor - Bing Ads Editor is a free downloadable application for managing Bing Ads advertising campaigns. It allows the advertiser to manage multiple accounts at the same time, make bulk changes, copy or move items between adgroups and campaigns, and more.

Bing Merchant Center - Bing Merchant Center is a tool that helps you upload your store and product data to Bing and make it available to Bing Shopping.

Black Hat SEO - The opposite of White Hat SEO, these Search Engine Optimization, or SEO, tactics are ways of tricking the Search Engines to get better rankings for a website. Black Hat SEO is a temporary tactic for increasing ranking, as search engine designers are constantly on the lookout for techniques that attempt to circumvent their algorithms. If not immediately, using black hat methods will eventually get your site drastically lower rankings or banned from the search engines altogether.

Blog - Short for Web log, blogs are part journal, part website. Typically the newest entry (blog post) appears at the top of the page with older entries coming after in reverse chronological order.

Bounce Rate - The percentage of people who visit your website but leave without visiting any other page.

Brand Stacking - Multiple page one listings from a single domain. Prior to 2010, a site would be fortunate if it had three first page results for branded searches. Since Google tweaked its algorithm to include Brand Stacking, that number has risen to as many as eight of the top search rankings

Broad Match - This is the default matching option. With this bid type your ad may show if a search term contains your keywords in any way. Your ads may show for synonyms of your keywords, related searches, and other relevant variations or phrases.

Buyer Persona - Fictional depictions of your target customers that serve as valuable points of reference for various digital marketing strategies. Marketing professionals take considerations from buyer goals, industry research, customer data, demographics, and natural human behaviors when forming buyer personas. The ultimate goal of this practice is to create an image of your ideal customer. That way, you can personalize your site layout, develop new content, or tailor any marketing strategies to increase the chances of acquiring the customers you need to grow your business.

Canonical Tag - A canonical tag tells (most) search engines which page is preferred when two URLs are similar or duplicate. In most instances this tag is used when you have products or content that is accessible by multiple URLs or in some cases, even websites. The tag is part of the HTML head code using the attribute *rel=canonical*.

Cascading Style Sheet (CSS) - Defines how HTML elements such as layout, colors, and fonts will be displayed. External style sheets can be stored in CSS files which allow for faster loading pages, smaller file sizes, and other benefits for visitors, search engines, and designers. A style sheet helps to maintain a unified look and feel, thus a more professional appearance throughout all pages of your web site.

ccTLD - **ccTLD**'s are "Country-code" TLD's showing what country a site is focused on or based in. Using Google and the United Kingdom as an example, Google UK is google.co.uk. Sometimes these ccTLD's are two sets of letters separated by a period (e.g. "co.uk" for the UK or "com.au" for Australia) and sometimes they are just one set of letters (e.g. ".fr" for France).

Click through Rate (CTR) – The formula (number of clicks) divided by (number of impressions) gives the click through rate, a common internet marketing measurement tool for ad effectiveness. This rate tells you how many times people are actually clicking on your ad out of the number of times your ad is shown.

Cloaking - Showing a search engine spider or bot one version of a Web page and a different version to the end user. Several search engines have explicit rules against unapproved cloaking.

Content Management System - Content Management Systems (CMS) allow website owners to make text and picture changes to their websites without specialized programming knowledge of software like Adobe Dreamweaver or Microsoft FrontPage. CMS examples include WordPress, Drupal, and Joomla.

Content Marketing - Content marketing is an inbound marketing practice that seeks to generate leads and traffic through the creation and distribution of content that caters to the needs of a defined audience of prospective customers. Content marketing as a strategy for SEO service providers achieved critical mass in the latter part of 2012 following the release of the Penguin algorithm update by Google, which adjusted a number of spam factors and affected a high percentage of search queries.

Content Network - Each major search engine offers a form of a content network within its paid search interface, typically referred to as content networks, although Google just renamed their content network the Google Display Network.

Content Tags - HTML tags such as Header and Alt Tags that define the essence of the content contained within them.

Contextual Advertising - A feature offered by major search engine advertisers allowing your advertisement to be placed next to related news articles and on other Web pages. Contextual advertising seeks to match Web content from the display page with your advertised search term(s).

Conversion Rate - This statistic, or metric, tells you what percentage of people is taking an action the advertiser defines as a conversion. A "conversion" may mean, for example, a sign-up for free information, a completed survey, or a purchase.

Conversion Rate Optimization - Depending on what your site deems as a conversion, there are steps that can always be taken to improve the likelihood that visitors to your site will perform a conversion driven action. Typically, this means changing certain aspects centered on the conversion. For example, if you have an ecommerce site, you may change the orientation of certain elements or their physical appearance like the color of the "Add to cart" button or removing certain steps to make it easier to purchase an item. Conversion rate optimization relies heavily on A/B testing as what may work for one website may not necessarily work for another.

Cookie - a small piece of data sent from a website and stored on the user's computer by the user's web browser while the user is browsing. Cookies were designed to be a reliable mechanism for websites to remember stateful information (such as items added in the shopping cart in an online store) or to record the user's browsing activity (including clicking particular buttons, logging in, or recording which pages were visited in the past). They can also be used to remember arbitrary pieces of information that the user previously entered into form fields such as names, addresses, passwords, and credit card numbers.

Cost per Acquisition (CPA) - An online advertising cost structure where you pay per an agreed-upon actionable event, such as a lead, registration, or sale.

Cost per Click (CPC) - A common way to pay for search engine and other types of online advertising, CPC means you pay a pre-determined amount each time someone clicks on your advertisement to visit your site. You usually set a top amount you are willing to pay per click for each search term, and the amount you pay will be equal to or less than that amount, depending on the particular search engine and your competitors' bids. Also referred to as Pay Per Click (PPC) or Paid Search Marketing.

Cost per Impression (CPM) - A common internet marketing cost structure, especially for banner advertising. You agree to pay a set cost for every 1,000 (M in Roman numerals) Impressions your ad receives.

Crawler - Component of a search engine that gathers listings by automatically "crawling" the Web. A search engine's crawler (also known as a Spider or robot) follows links to Web Pages. It makes copies of those pages and stores them in a search engine's index.

Customer Relationship Management (CRM) - Software solutions that help enterprise businesses manage customer relationships in an organized way. An example of a CRM would be a database containing detailed customer information that management and salespeople can reference in order to match customer needs with products, inform customers of service requirements, etc.

D

Day Parting - Day parting refers to serving ads at different times of the day and days of the week, or even changing bids or ad copy at different times. For example, you may not want your ads to show from 11AM-2PM on Tuesdays. This can be done manually in most online platforms, or automatically in some such as Google AdWords.

Description Tags - HTML tags that provide a brief description of your site search engines can understand. Description tags should contain the main keywords of the page it is describing in a short summary.

Display URL - The URL displayed along with your ads. This URL can vary from the Destination URL, but must use the same root domain.

Directories - A type of search engine where business listings are gathered through submissions, information pulled from data aggregators (e.g. Acxiom), or a combination of the two. Websites are often reviewed and placed in a relevant category. Directories can be utilized for strengthening local SEO and providing relevant referral traffic.

Domain Authority - Developed by Moz (Moz.com), domain authority is a score ranging from 0 – 100 that predicts how a website will rank on search engines. It is often used by SEOs to compare one site to another as well as tracking the improvement over time.

Domain Name - A website's main address.

Doorway Page - A Web page created to rank well in a search engine's organic listings (non-paid) and typically delivers very little information to those viewing it.

Domain Name Monitoring - Monitoring Domains across various extensions. For example, a monitoring service may keep metrics on the domains MyName.com, MyName.net, and MyName.Biz.

Drip Marketing - marketing communications that are written in advance of delivery, and then sent to prospective customers or current customers at pre-determined intervals in their buyer or customer journey.

Dynamic Retargeting - Ads shown to users who have already been to your site. These ads typically contain images and information about the previous item viewed.

E

EdgeRank - The algorithm Facebook uses to rank business / brand pages, groups, celebrity pages or individual accounts to determine which posts from those accounts will appear in the Newsfeed of users connected to those pages and profiles (or pages and profiles tagged in the posts).

E-Marketing - Another synonym for online marketing, internet marketing, or digital marketing. Marketing strategies (like SEO, PPC, retargeting, social advertising, etc.) that are deployed using web based technology in an effort to generate sales leads or e-commerce revenue.

Enhanced Bidding - A feature specific to Google AdWords. When you select to utilize enhanced bidding, you're giving AdWords the power to adjust your bidding in order to increase conversions.

Exact Match – Refers to keyword search matching. This is the most specific of the match types. With this type your ad or page will only show if the user's search term contains your keywords exactly as they are written.

Expanded Text Ads - Text ads with double the characters compared with standard text ads. The ad format (today) is composed of two 30-character headline fields, one 80-caracter description field and two 15-character paths in the display URL field. ETAs are mobile-optimized, so you can reach potential customers on desktop and mobile devices with the same ad.

f

Final URL - The URL address for the page to which you're sending traffic from your ads.

Folksonomy - also known as social tagging, is a user-defined metadata collection. Users do not deliberately create folksonomies and there is rarely a prescribed purpose, but a folksonomy evolves when many users create or store content at particular sites and identify what they think the content is about.

Forum - A place on the internet where people with common interests or backgrounds come together to find information and discuss topics.

G

Geo-Targeting - The ability to reach potential clients by their physical location. All the major search engines offer the ability to geo-target searches in their Pay-Per-Click campaigns by viewing their IP addresses. Geo-targeting allows advertisers to specify markets by regions as far as IP address can identify them.

Gmail Sponsored Promotions (GSP) - Google Display Network campaigns that allow advertisers to show ads in Gmail. The advertiser pays when someone clicks to expand the ad in their inbox.

Graphical Search Inventory - Banners and other types of advertising units that can be synchronized to search keywords. Includes pop-ups browser toolbars and rich media.

Growth Hacking – Not a specific technology, but a way to increase customer acquisition using the most effective tactics available to engage a specific buyer persona. Typically deployed in the "Software as a Service" industry or startup environments, growth hacking often involves multiple marketing strategies and nimble product development practices to create a solution that rapidly scales the user base of a product/service.

H

Hashtag - Formerly called the 'pound sign', this symbol (#) is used on social media (primarily Instagram and Twitter), as a way to group tweets or pictures by category or phrase. The '#' is placed directly, without space, in front of the text to be marked.

Header (or Heading) Tags () - HTML heading and subheading tags are critical components of search engine marketing, as often times both are graphical, thereby unreadable to search engine spiders. Optimally, page titles should also be included to clearly define the page's purpose and theme. All of the header tags should be used according to their relevance, with more prominent titles utilizing <h1> (heading 1), <h2> (subheading), and so on to <h6>.

HTML - HyperText Markup Language, the programming language used in websites. Developers use other languages that can be read and understood by HTML to expand what they can do on the Web (e.g., Java, Javascript).

Hyperlink - Typically blue and underlined, hyperlinks, commonly called "links" for short, allow the user to navigate to other pages on the Web with a click of the mouse.

I

Image Maps - Clickable regions, hyperlinks, within images displayed on a web page. Image maps enable search engine spiders to "read" this material.

Impressions - The number of times someone views a page displaying your ad. Note that this is not the same as actually seeing your ad, making placement and an understanding of the site's traffic particularly important when paying on a Cost per 1,000 Impressions basis.

Inbound or Incoming Links - See Backlinks

Inbound Marketing - Marketing services and strategies that successfully cause prospective customers to navigate to a website on their own accord, usually due to the consistent creation of engaging content. Examples include SEO, content marketing, blogging, and email marketing to a list that is self-curated. This is in contrast to traditional advertising methods that get the attention of prospective customers through paid advertising promotions.

Index - The collection of information a search engine has which searchers can query against. With crawler-based search engines, the index is typically copies of all the Web pages they have found from crawling the Web. With human-powered directories, the index contains the summaries of all the websites that have been categorized.

Internet Marketing – A catch-all phrase that includes any of a number of ways to reach internet users, including Search Engine Marketing, Search Engine Optimization, and Banner advertising.

Internal Linking - Placing hyperlinks on a page to other pages within the same site. This helps users find more information, improve site interaction, and enhances your SEO efforts.

Interstitial - An ad that appears between two pages a person is trying to view. The ad often appears near a hyperlink allowing someone to quit viewing your ad and go directly to the page he or she originally tried to access.

J

JavaScript - Not to be confused with its distant cousin Java, Javascript is an Object Oriented Programming language developed by NetScape. It provides enhanced functionality over and above the capabilities of HTML.

K

Keyword - Almost interchangeable with Search Term, keywords are words or a group of words that a person may search for in a Search Engine. Keywords also refer to the terms you bid on through search engine marketing in trying to attract visitors to your website or Landing Page.

Keyword Difficulty - A metric commonly used in search engine optimization that determines how much on-page targeting and offsite link building will be required to rank for a phrase. Also commonly referred to as KPI, most tools that monitor keyword difficulty use a percentage scale of 1-100, with phrases ranked in descending order.

Keyword Stuffing - When the Web was young and search engines were starting to gain in popularity, some smart website owners realized that the search engine algorithms responded better to some meta tags than others, so they started overusing these keywords, often with high search volumes and no relevancy to the site, into the title, description, and keyword tags.

Keyword Tags - HTML tags that define the keywords used on web pages.

L

Landing Page - The first page a person sees when coming to your website from an advertisement.

Link Building - The process of obtaining hyperlinks (links or backlinks) from one website back to your own.

Link Juice - SEO term referring to the equity passed to a site via links (either internal or external). High authority, high traffic sites have more link juice, which will more positively affect your rankings, than a low authority, low traffic site. The more link juice your site has, the more positively the search engines will view it.

Link Popularity - How many websites link to yours, how popular those linking sites are, and how much their content relates to yours. Link popularity is an important part of Search Engine Optimization, which also values the sites that you link out to.

Link Reclamation - This is when outreach is performed to earn backlinks to your site. The situations in which this occur can be if your domain name changes, a re-branding occurs, or when your brand is mentioned online (in an article, blog post, etc.) and there is no link from the mention going back to your website.

Local Search - A huge and growing portion of the search engine marketing industry. Local search allows users to find businesses and websites within a specific geographic range. This includes local search features on search engines and online yellow page sites. Optimizing for local search requires different practices than for traditional Search Engine Optimization.

Long Tail Keywords - a keyword phrase that contains at least three words (though some say two or more is considered long-tail). Long-tail keywords are used to target niche demographics rather than mass audiences. In other words, they're more specific and often less competitive than generic keyword terms.

Marketing Automation - Software suites that combine a variety of popular online marketing strategies like email, social media, CRM and SEO into one platform. In addition to efficient and automatic completion of a variety of marketing tasks, these applications also allow marketing teams to view a more direct correlation between their efforts and ROI from online marketing.

Meta Search Engine - A search engine that gets listings from two or more other search engines rather than crawling the Web itself.

Meta Tags - (see also keyword tags, description tags etc.) – Meta tags allow you to highlight important Keywords related to your site in a way that matters to Search Engines, but that your website visitors typically do not see. Examples of meta tags include Header Tags and Alt Tags.

Microblogging - Microblogging refers to platforms allowing you to post information in snippets of 140 characters at a time via phone or web. Twitter is the preeminent example of a microblogging site, although there are many others, such as Gab (Gab.ai).

Microsites - a site created by a business or online publisher, for a specific purpose, that functions independently from the primary website of the business/publisher. Microsites are typically created for events, specialized topics or services, or for content created for a specific topic.

Mobile Enabled Website: Also called Mobile Optimized Website. This is a version of your website that is built to display correctly on internet enabled smart phones such as the iPhone. Mobile Optimized Websites offer an easier to read and navigate platform for users and scales down images for viewing on a smaller screen.

Mobile-Friendly - A site that is optimized for mobile users. The text and images must be able to be viewed on a display on a mobile device while still being functional and user-friendly.

n

Natural Listings - Also referred to as "organic results", these are the non-advertised listings in Search Engines.

Naver - Naver is Korea's largest search engine and Web property.

Neuromarketing - A field of marketing that incorporates neuroscience as a means of predicting consumer behavior.

o

Opt-in - This type of registration requires a person submitting information to specifically request he or she be contacted or added to a list.

Organic Listings - See Natural Listings.

Outbound Links - Links on any web page leading to another web page, whether they are within the same site or another website.

p

PageRank - PageRank is a value that Google assigns for pages and websites that it indexes, based on all the factors in its algorithm. Google does release an external PageRank scoring pages from 1-10 that you can check for any website, but this external number is not the same as the internal PageRank Google uses to determine search engine results. All independent search engines have their own version of PageRank. Potentially interesting fact: PageRank was named for Google's Larry Page and it is calculated at the page level – pun fun!

Paid Inclusion - Advertising program where pages are guaranteed to be included in a search engine's index in exchange for payment.

Paid Listings - Listings that search engines sell to advertisers, usually through paid placement or paid inclusion programs. Contrast with organic (natural) listings.

Paid Search - Also referred to as Paid Placement, Pay Per Click, and sometimes Search Engine Marketing, paid search marketing allows advertisers to pay to be listed within the Search Engine Results Pages for specific keywords or phrases.

Pay-for-Performance - Term popularized by search engines as a synonym for pay-per-click, stressing to advertisers that they are only paying for ads that 'perform' in terms of delivering traffic, as opposed to CPM-based ads, which cost money, even if they don't generate a click.

Pay per Click (PPC) - a business model whereby a company that has placed an advertisement on a website pays a sum of money to the host website when a user clicks on to the advertisement.

Permission Marketing - focuses on receiving the consent of users before being contacted or, in some cases, even seeing an advertisement (see also Opt-in). Permission marketing is centered on the concept that people are increasingly tuning out the barrage of advertisements they see each day. Its focal tenet is that a business will have a better chance of gaining a client when the client first gives permission to be sent an ad or contacted.

Phrase Match - This match type is more specific than broad, but not as specific as exact. This bid type allows your ads to show for phrases that exactly contain your keywords or are close variations.

Pop-Under - An advertisement that opens in a new Web Browser window once you visit a particular page or take some other action. Considered less annoying than Pop-Up ads because the new window appears behind the existing one.

Pop-Up - An ad or web page that opens a new window on your screen that partially or wholly covers your current web browser window.

Push Notifications - are messages that pop up on mobile devices, that originate from a specific app or server. It's not necessary to be using your mobile devices, or even be in the app, to receive push notifications. They act as a way to keep the user engaged with the app, and hopefully take action (ex: send a coupon, event notification, etc.).

Query - Query is another term for "keyword" or "search term." Within Google AdWords, search query reports show the actual terms that searchers used to click on your ads, as opposed to the advertised keyword that is in your account. These two sets of words may or may not be the same.

R

RSS Feed - Real Simple Syndication (RSS), also Rich Site Summary, originally RDF Site Summary; often called Really Simple Syndication, is a type of web feed that allows users to access updates to online content in a standardized, computer-readable format.

Reciprocal Link - A link exchange between two sites. Both sites will display a link to the other site somewhere on their pages. This type of link is generally much less desirable than a one-way inbound link.

Remarketing - Remarketing is Google AdWords's term for retargeting.

Responsive Ads - Responsive ads automatically adjust their size, appearance, and format to fit just about any available ad space. For example, your responsive ad might show as a native banner ad on one site and a dynamic text ad on another, as it automatically transforms itself to fit precisely where you need it to go to meet your advertising goals.

Retargeting – Directing advertising to a person based on information about sites he or she has previously visited. When a user performs an action (e.g., a visit to a site or a search) a cookie may be placed on his or her browser. As the user visits other sites, advertising, such as a banner or other type of display ad, is shown on their display based on information stored in the cookie.

Return on Investment (ROI) - A performance measure used to evaluate the efficiency of an investment or to compare the efficiency of a number of different investments. ROI measures the amount of return on an investment relative to the investment's cost. To calculate ROI, the benefit (or return) of an investment is divided by the cost of the investment, and the result is expressed as a percentage or a ratio.

Rich Media - Web advertisements or pages that are more animated and/or interactive than static Banners or pages.

Robot or Bot - See Crawler.

Robots.txt - A file used to keep Web pages from being indexed or to tell which pages you want a search engine to index.

Root Domain - The term root domain means different things depending on whether it refers to the Internet as a whole or a specific website. Your root domain commonly means the highest level of hierarchy for the website you control. MyName.com is the root domain for MyName.com/Blog, MyName.com/Store Front, MyName.com/About, etc.

Run of Site (ROS) - A contract specifying Run of Site means that a Banner or other type of online advertisement can appear on any page, and usually in any open placement, of a particular website.

S

Schema Markup - a piece of code added to a page's HTML code to help search engines understand what your website is about and what type of information it contains.

Scraping - The process of copying content from one Web property and using it on another. In other words, stealing. Scraping technologies have evolved because of the needs for current, relevant content and to stay ahead of legitimate content creators trying to protect what they've written.

Search Engine Optimization (SEO) – Using writing and programming techniques to make a site more "search engine friendly." The end result is making a site appear higher in search engine rankings.

Search Engine Reputation Management (SERM) - This allows a person or organization better positioning through strategy involving Search Engine Optimization, Paid Search Marketing, Press Optimization, Blogging, and Social Media.

Search Engine Results Page - Search Engine Results Pages, or SERPs, are the Web pages displayed by any Search Engine for any given search. They display both Natural (organic) Listings and Pay-Per-Click ads. How high you are listed and where your ad is shown depends on Search Engine Optimization; and paid Search Engine Marketing respectively.

Search Retargeting - A specific type of retargeting that allows an advertiser to show ads to searchers of given keywords who have never visited the advertiser's site.

SEM - An acronym for Search Engine Marketing and may also be used to refer to a person or company that does Search

Engine Marketing – either paid search, search engine optimization, or both.

SEO - An acronym for Search Engine Optimization and may also be used to refer to a person or company that does search engine optimization.

Shopping Ads - Formerly known as Product Listing Ads (PLAs), these ads appear in both Google and Bing search results as images of individual products above the search results. These ads are specifically for eCommerce companies and instead of using keywords, ads are triggered by searches containing words in the product's title, description, or attributes.

Signature –A few lines of default text that can be customized and added to all outgoing email messages from a personal email account.

Site Retargeting - The most common form of retargeting, this refers to displaying your ads to a visitor based on a visit to your site, or individual page of your site. These cookie-based ads can appear on any publisher's page throughout the ad network being used. Various targeting options exist, including only showing ads when a certain page has been visited (such as a landing page) and an action has not been completed (e.g. a conversion).

Social Commerce - Selling goods directly online through social media channels. As "electronic commerce" was shortened to "eCommerce", social commerce is sometimes shortened to "sCommerce" or "fCommerce," the latter being short for "Facebook commerce."

Social Media - A type of online media where information is uploaded primarily through user submission. Web surfers are no longer simply consumers of content, but active content publishers. Many different forms of social media exist including more established formats like forums and blogs, and newer formats such as wikis, podcasts, social networking, image and video sharing, and virtual reality.

Social Media Marketing (SMM) - An online marketing mix that utilizes the different strategies available through social networking sites to promote a product or service.

Social Networking - A type of social media, social networking websites allow users to interact and create or change content on the site. These sites, which businesses are now using for marketing purposes, allow users to create their own websites and/or online spheres (e.g. LinkedIn and Facebook), share photographs (e.g. Flickr), microblog small bits of information to their personal community (e.g. Twitter) or recommend information for others to find on the Internet (e.g. del.icio.us and Digg). The sites in this last grouping are also referred to as social bookmarking or social news sites. There are also a growing number of sites that are heavily dependent on mobile and geographic locations, such as foursquare.

Spam - Can refer to unwanted data sent via email or put on a website to game a search engine. Spam to a search engine is Web content that the search engine deems to be detrimental to its efforts to deliver relevant, quality search results.

Spider – As a spider might crawl over a web, World Wide Web spiders "crawl" this web to find all the linked pages of a website to gather information to include the site in their natural listings and to determine each site's ranking vis-a-vis various search terms.

Stickiness - How often people return to a website. Constant updates, news feeds, and exclusive content are all ways to make a site stickier.

Structured Snippets - These ad extensions allow your ads to highlight specific aspects of products and services. They provide context on the nature and variety of your products and services before visitors click through to your site.

Subdomain - Also referred to as a 3rd level domain is very simply, a domain that is part of a higher domain in web hierarchy. Subdomains can be created at any time with no limit and without a registrar. A common reason to create subdomains would be to differentiate a sector of your business such as "info.yoursite.com" or "tools.yoursite.com."

Submission - The act of submitting a URL for inclusion into a search engine's index. Unless done through paid inclusion, submission generally does not guarantee listing. In addition, submission does not help with rank improvement on crawler-based search engines unless search engine optimization efforts have been undertaken. Submission can be done manually (i.e., you can fill out an online form and submit) or automated, where a software program or online service may process the forms behind the scenes.

Subpage - A page that appears below the top-level pages in a website's navigation. These pages often appear as drop downs in a top navigation bar or sidebar menu. Think of subpages as "child pages" of the "parent page."

T

Tags - Words or phrases used to describe and categorize individual blog posts, videos, and pictures. Correctly using tags organizes content for users and can help with visibility through SEO and social media optimization.

Takeover Ads - A type of display advertising typically reserved for high profile brands and products (consumer goods, new mass media releases, sporting events) on high traffic online publications. Commonly referenced on the homepages of sites like Yahoo!, MSN, or even ESPN.com, this advertising strategy is often called a "homepage takeover."

Targeting - Shaping internet marketing campaigns to attract certain specific groups of prospective clients. Examples of groups that might be targeted include women, gun owners, and Medicare recipients. Behavioral Targeting is a newer, specific type of focus for advertisers.

Topic Modeling - An SEO strategy used when creating or optimizing content based on the primary keyword selected for a page. This is done by identifying keywords related to the same subject of the primary keyword and utilizing these as secondary keywords. Content is then optimized around the new keywords, achieving a higher level of SEO.

Text Ad - An online advertisement that contains only written copy. Paid listings found on the results pages of the main Search Engines are currently Text Ads.

Three Way Linking - A link building strategy designed to create two one-way links between sites that want to complete a link exchange. When using this link-building tactic, one website owner involved in the exchange of links typically has access to more than one property. After adding an external link from one site (in this example, "Site A") to another destination ("Site B"), then Site B places an external link to a third domain ("Site C"). Therefore, a three way link exchange is completed when Site A links to Site B, and Site B links to Site C.

TLD - Top Level Domain. The last segment of a domain name, or the part that follows immediately after the "dot" symbol. TLDs are mainly classified into two categories: generic TLDs and country-specific TLDs. Examples of some of the popular TLDs include .com, .org, .net, .gov, .biz and .edu.

Tracking Code - Information typically included in the URL that allows an advertiser to track the effectiveness of various aspects of an advertisement. Commonly tracked items include Search Term and referring Search Engine.

TrueView Ads - A video ad created in Google AdWords. TrueView video ads come in two formats: in-stream and in-display. In-Stream ads appear before videos on YouTube (owned by Google) and the Display Network. In-display ads can appear in YouTube search results, videos, or on partner websites.

Twitter Retargeting - Twitter Tailored Audiences are used to create retargeting campaigns that can serve ads to people who have previously interacted with your brand.

U

URL - Uniform Resource Locator. These are the letters and symbols that make up the address of specific Web pages, e.g., http://www.demarsouthard.com.

Unique Value Proposition (UVP) - In essence, what it is that sets your product, service, or company apart from others.

Universal Search - The placement of multiple types of results within a general search so that a user receives images, videos, local search results, news articles, and more next to general Web pages. Also called blended search.

Usability – A measure of how easy it is for a user to navigate a website and find the information he or she is seeking.

User-Generated Content - Brands with a dedicated audience will sometimes try to include them in the content creation process. Known as user-generated content, or "UGC," users or community members of a brand will create and contribute their original content for the brand. This content is usually posted via social media or directly on the brand's website.

V

Video Marketing - An online marketing strategy that leverages the consumption of videos by internet users to promote a brand, product, or service.

Viral Marketing - A newer method of internet marketing that attempts to make advertisements so interesting that viewers will pass them along via social networking sites to others free of charge to the advertisers.

Web 2.0 - Web 2.0 was never clearly defined, but focuses on several major themes, including AJAX, social networking, folksonomies, lightweight collaboration, social bookmarking, and media sharing. Wikis and user-edited search all operate under this premise.

Web 3.0 – Not completely accepted by the industry, this term refers to the third generation of web technology, focusing on innovation in back-end infrastructure. It is expected that this cycle will continue for five to ten years, and will result in making the Web more connected, more open, and more intelligent. The term was coined first by John Markoff of the *New York Times*.

Web Browser - An application used to access the internet. Common browsers include Microsoft Internet Explorer (IE), Apple's Safari, and Mozilla Firefox, and Google Chrome.

Webinar - "Web Seminar". These virtual seminars allow people from anywhere in the world to attend via an internet connection. They offer tremendous opportunities for businesses to reach out to people over large geographic areas at low costs.

Web Metrics - See Analytics.

White Hat SEO - Used to describe certain Search Engine Optimization (SEO) methods, being "white hat" means using only SEO techniques that are completely above board and accepted by the Search Engines.

WordPress - WordPress is an extremely popular Content Management System. Developed originally for blogs, WordPress offers a great degree of flexibility and functionality.

WYSIWYG – Acronym for "*What You See Is What You Get*". Usually refers to an interface where you can edit a file, whether it's an email message or a brochure. "A WYSIWYG interface".

X

XML - Extensible Markup Language. Content developers use this language with a variety of forms of content, including text, audio, and visual in order to allow users to define their own elements.

Y

Yandex - Yandex is a search engine serving primarily Russia and other countries formerly part of the Soviet Union. They also offer a Google AdWords-like paid search program, Yandex Direct.

Thank you for reading *Internet Profit System*. If you enjoyed this eBook and found it helpful, you might also want to check out other Internet marketing eBooks that will be available in the near future at Amazon.com by this same author.

Wishing you the best in your life and business,

Justin Southworth

www.ingramcontent.com/pod-product-compliance
Lightning Source LLC
Chambersburg PA
CBHW070155230526
45471CB00002B/672